Helenio Barbetta   Kurt Stapelfeldt

Homes decorated by nature

PLANTS, ART AND MATERIAL

Lannoo

8 Introduction

14 Plants and Flowers

18 Wrap-around sunroom
28 Compact, deliberate and vibrant
36 Wunderkammer
44 The old, the new and the view
56 Inner-city time capsule
66 Reinforcing the roots
74 An architect's home

84 Art and Decoration

88 Invasion of the flying lampshades
98 Lucky number 40
106 Escape to the country
118 The secret garden
128 Big, bold & beautiful
138 The return of the native
146 Sofia's choice
156 Conserving tradition

166 Materials and Textures

170 A surprising country home
182 Mid-century California style
194 The perfect second home
204 The stage is set
214 Lord of the manor
222 Urban oasis
232 Renovated farmhouse
240 Bohemian atmosphere
248 Brought back to life

INTRODUCTION

From the time our species first learned to walk upright, we have been in search of a safe place to lay our heads when the sun goes down or when we need to protect ourselves against the weather. Our home is our refuge. It is where our children sleep and where we nourish our bodies. It can be heaven and can also sometimes be hell, but we always return home. It can be a place of functionality and basic necessities, and your house can speak volumes about who you are. The choices you make in building or decorating your home are deeply personal and can reflect either who you are right now or who you aspire to be, and, most importantly, what your priorities are.

In this book is a collection of homes photographed over a long career by Helenio Barbetta. The pictures are a testament to the homeowners who made intentional decisions to create a personalised environment which is a reflection of themselves. When nature is important to you in everyday life, it will be ever-present in your home. Whether in the countryside of Liguria or in the city centre of Madrid, the homes shown here are an expression of our innate need to have nature close to us.

Whether in the form of potted plants, floral patterns or rough-hewn oak-wood flooring, bringing nature into our living spaces is a choice. As an interior designer, I have had the privilege of accompanying so many wonderful people on their journey to surround themselves with the objects they love, the items which best tell their story. When interacting with a space, we first allow nature in through the windows, the copious amount of natural light flooding in. It is sunlight which is the most important component of nature, and so every morning when we open the shutters or the blinds, it is sunlight which blesses our day, which feeds our plants and which, over time, will bleach your overexposed sofa! So, whether your own home is as studied as the ones in this book or is a college dorm room with an overwatered cactus, every home starts the day kissed by nature.

This collection of homes inspired by nature takes a broad view of how nature is expressed within the living space, and is divided into three chapters: 'Art and Decoration', 'Plants and Flowers' and, lastly, 'Materials and Texture'. They are groupings which best represent the approach of each homeowner to connect themselves with the aspects of nature they find most important. For some it is oversized prints of tropical leaves, while for others it is a picture window looking out over the Italian countryside, and for still others it is a ficus poking its branches out from behind a pillar. All of the living situations are different, as are the contexts in which they are found, but in this book there is a commonality between the homes: the love of nature and the need to bring it inside, giving it a new expression and enriching the lives of those who remain close to it.

Plants and Flowers

CHAPTER ONE

'To plant a garden is to believe in tomorrow.'

– AUDREY HEPBURN

Gone are the days when you would go to smell your grandmother's flowers only to realise they were made of plastic and fabric. Today, we want to fill our homes with the real thing – living, breathing plants that can often complete a room as much as artworks on the wall. The houses in this chapter use indoor plants as a conduit to the nature outside. They are smaller, contained and manageable houseplants, perfect for those who do not have a garden but still want to add greenery. Being close to these plants somehow manages to soothe the soul and lighten the mood. They require quality sunlight, and in the act of providing that for the plants, we can benefit from that light too.

Wrap-around sunroom

HOMEOWNERS
Stefania Agostini and Luca Mostarda
(AMArchitecture)

Living and working with your spouse can be challenging, but it is not without its success stories – Charles and Ray Eames immediately come to mind. This is what Milanese couple Stefania Agostini and Luca Mostarda undertook when they opened their studio AMArchitecture after both graduated from the Accademia di Architettura in Mendrisio, Switzerland, launching their practice in 2017. They focused their work mainly on renovations and the production of design products. While their business blossomed, so did their home life, with the births of three-year-old Agnese and one-year-old Matilde. To accommodate their growing family, the two architects began the renovation of a city apartment that had a former life as offices. The challenge was to break out from the long corridor layout, best suited to a workplace, to create a functional and contemporary family home.

To renovate the space, they made bold decisions that transformed it into a greenhouse, isolated from the noise and pollution of the city. Another challenge was being on the first floor of a busy street. To achieve the feeling of being in a greenhouse, they constructed a second row of windows, forming a sunroom that wraps around the living room and kitchen area. Within these spaces, a flowerbed nurtures perennial plants, such as *Ficus robusta, Ficus lyrata, Ficus elastica, Sansevieria, Palma areca, Philodendron selloum, Aglaonema crispum, Calathea makoyana, Aloe vera, Aechmea fasciata* and more, all of which absorb pollution. The greenery serves as a natural filter, purifying both incoming and outgoing air, while the dual sequence of windows creates a serene environment. 'Our love for nature and understanding of the importance of sustainability,' explain the architects, 'are part of our generation, and now with us being parents of two girls, it has made us even more aware of these issues.'

A focal point of this indoor potted forest is the kitchen, slightly raised from the living room, making it prominent. As Stefania says, 'It is very nice to cook while observing what is happening around you from above. We also covered it with bronzed mirrors to make it more luxurious: we love reflective surfaces because they create special lighting effects.' With a portion of the floor space being used by the greenhouse, space-efficient solutions had to be found, like in the long dark corridor. It was removed where the girls' room is, opening up large arches that create an indoor porch, adding light and enlarging the space. The couple has used natural materials like unfinished wood and marble and made use of a vibrant modern palette. This home is now a testament to the love that grows within it, just like the plants. Love is even in the name of the studio, AMArchitecture – *ama* is the third-person singular of 'to love' in Italian.

18 Plants and Flowers

'We love reflective surfaces because they create special lighting effects.'

– STEFANIA & LUCA

Homes Decorated by Nature

Compact, deliberate and vibrant

HOMEOWNERS
Christian Frascaro
and Francesco Cristiano

Milan is the capital of the Italian region of Lombardy and has long represented the economic heart of the country. Headquarters, factories and studios dictate world trends for the coming years, attracting creative professionals to the city in search of opportunities. This results in a high number of former office buildings being converted to apartments in very interesting neighbourhoods. Christian Frascaro and Francesco Cristiano have created a home in one of these former offices that displays an elegance and taste well beyond their years. The couple, two dynamic individuals with a bustling schedule, are fuelled by youth, creativity and diverse interests. Hailing from Apulia, Christian immerses himself in the world of luxury hotels, drawing inspiration from architecture and design. On the other hand, Naples-born Francesco, a visual merchandiser, exudes a passion for art, fashion and photography. United by a keen aesthetic sense and a vibrant imagination, the couple bring a unique blend of talents and perspectives to their endeavours.

'With this project, we have officially entered the world of interior design,' the couple proudly comments. 'It all started from an old office on the first floor of a 1970s building, located a short distance from the Monumental Cemetery. It has all the charm and is in a strategic position between the Isola and Garibaldi districts, so it's super-connected to the city centre. Initially, we were looking for something that could be redone from scratch, possibly on a higher floor, perhaps even with a small outdoor area. But then unexpectedly, during the site inspection, these rooms won us over for the natural light that generously entered from the large windows.' The entire floor plan has been reimagined, and although it is only 50 square metres, the couple has created a beautiful and functional contemporary home. The one-time executive office is now a spacious living room, and the storage room is now a small kitchen and a bedroom. The only space left in the original position is the bathroom, which underwent a major restyle. Bringing some nature into the well-lit rooms was important for the couple, who both hail from coastal regions with often immediate access to nature. They aimed to introduce as much greenery as possible into their home. Francesco and Christian find delight in the artful fusion of vintage pieces and modern creations. Their design ethos seamlessly blends classic elements with exotic details, drawing inspiration from the Bauhaus movement and the teachings of influential masters. Gio Ponti and Ludwig Mies van der Rohe are among their favourites. Their artistic influences extend beyond borders, incorporating elements from China and Morocco, a testament to the cultural richness gathered from their travels in the quest for fresh inspiration.

Homes Decorated by Nature

'These rooms won us over because of the natural light that generously enters through the large windows.'

– CHRISTIAN & FRANCESCO

Wunderkammer

HOMEOWNER
Arianna Bartolomeo
and Nicola Tamiozzo

It's always great to see a young couple building a home together with a clear vision of what they like and want. When you add an inspired emerging designer who also happens to be a good friend, the result is a home like this one in the city of Vicenza in northern Italy. Arianna and Nicola are a creative couple in search of an atmosphere reflective of their love for the exotic, the eclectic and everything remote in space and time. 'This house is our very own *Wunderkammer*. We live surrounded by elements that inspire and motivate us – colours, objects and wonders found during our travels or while browsing in the region's many vintage markets,' they explain. Arianna works in communications, and Nicola is a musician. They were looking for an early twentieth-century home, which they found on a historic street in Vicenza, just outside the city walls in a neighbourhood with a strong influence from the Liberty (Italian art nouveau) movement. They had found their 'place to be', surrounded by villas from the early 1900s and lush gardens populated with palms and magnolias.

Enter Giacomo Totti, a close friend and interior designer. Arianna and Nicola explain: 'In addition to the long-standing friendship between us, there is a communion of tastes and interests. We discussed some ideas that we had developed over time, and he helped us to realize them and blend them into a coherent design concept. All that he proposed to us fully reflected our taste and our aesthetics. Just like him, we are crazy about the original, mainly Italian design pieces of the 1960s and 70s – Ponti, De Carli, Castiglioni, Munari, Bellini, Frattini and Buffa.' The layout of the home is filled with airy open spaces, giving them the possibility to create several different *Wunderkammern*, while restoring the original features to their former glory. As the couple says, 'The house is 110 square metres with a dual exposure: the kitchen, bedroom and bathroom face east, and the living room, dining room and study face west, with the rooms radiating out around a large central corridor. It is very bright, thanks to the numerous windows, two of which have balconies. We wanted the chromatic choices to dictate a certain mood, so we designed a palette inspired by the colours found in nature, warm and earthy, as opposed to the colder tones of green and sky blue.' To make the most of the available sunlight, the couple has filled the home with potted plants like palms and cacti. Where nature cannot be present, it is represented, like the jungle-themed tapestry above the master bed or the copper leaf motif over the fireplace. As the couple says, 'We have created similarities and contrasts between original vintage furniture from the 1960s and 70s, bespoke pieces by Giacomo Totti, pre-existences of the Liberty era and contemporary works of art by local designers. Each object tells us its story and has a different origin.'

Homes Decorated by Nature

'We live surrounded by elements that inspire and motivate us – colours, objects and wonders found during our travels or while browsing in the region's many vintage markets.'

– ARIANNA & NICOLA

40   Plants and Flowers

The old, the new and the view

HOMEOWNER
Alessandro Di Ruocco

At the heart of the Chiaia a Mare district in Naples, amid the vibrant intersection of tourism, fashion, culture and nightlife, lies a residence on Via Filangieri. To the south, the vast gulf unfolds, while to the north, history weaves its rich tapestry. This fourth-floor haven in a nineteenth-century building, meticulously restored by architect Giuliano Andrea dell'Uva, offers a captivating dance between sea and land. Once a baroque fortress that hosted the likes of Casanova, Goethe, Tasso and Caravaggio, Palazzo Cellammare stands as a testament to history, visible from the terrace that graces the residence. It's a view that constantly shifts perspectives – from the iconic Mount Vesuvius and the Lungomare di Napoli seen through the windows to the ever-changing postcard views of Naples framed in each room. Here, a young entrepreneur, Alessandro Di Ruocco, entrusted dell'Uva with the task of breathing new life into his home. The brief to dell'Uva was clear: 'I want an open home with retro atmospheres and spaces designed for hosting.'

Dell'Uva, an architect with vast experience of restoring historical homes, embraced the challenge. His task was to respect the genius loci, preserving the traces of memory while updating rooms and proportions. 'The context is elegant but not solemn. The layout is multifaceted, with a horizontal connotation,' notes dell'Uva. 'Some changes were inevitable, like connecting the living room and the dining room with the terrace and rethinking the kitchen, transforming it into an iron-and-glass box, completely exposed. Where time has erased, we have rebuilt, especially the plaster that we artfully peeled away in search of the original lime colours. In period houses, I always look for what is under the layers of paint. Here, a cloudy blue-grey has resurfaced with a high plinth in Pompeian red. The restorers from the Superintendency worked on it like a painting until the old and the new were homogenised. They usually work on paintings – even Caravaggio – but I involved them in this very special project.' The large terrace, once a somewhat overlooked space, now stands as an open-air room, seamlessly connected to the living room. Dell'Uva's decorative staircase, an intricate design of thin lacquered-iron panels, serves as both a screen and a balustrade. Ascending, the panoramic view unfolds, stretching as far as Capri. Inside, the decor is a curated blend of made-to-measure furniture, contemporary designer pieces and twentieth-century furnishings. The juxtapositions are deliberate, harmonising the styles of Robin Day and Alvar Aalto, Vico Magistretti and Piero Lissoni, Jaime Hayon and Le Corbusier.

'I want an open home with retro atmospheres and spaces designed for hosting.'

– ALESSANDRO

Homes Decorated by Nature

Homes Decorated by Nature

Inner-city time capsule

HOMEOWNERS
Laura Calevo and
Francesco and baby Folco

The city of Milan suffered some of Italy's heaviest bombing during World War II, which led to a post-war construction boom. One of the more interesting housing developments from the late 1960s was in Via Muratori, an innovative multi-use complex designed by the Roman Studio Passarelli in 1967. The architecture is what won over Laura Calevo and her husband Francesco, as they explain: 'The architectural qualities immediately won us over. The home has a strong characteristic language with a robust personality, appreciable through its details and the extensive study behind the original project, even at a conceptual level. We were impressed by the use of materials such as concrete, iron, glass and brick, combined with skill, resulting in a harmonious and elegant final effect. The layout of the interior spaces is simply perfect. The views are unique, with windows on all sides, overlooking a very pleasant garden. In a city like Milan, witnessing glimpses of oaks, limes and maples changing colours through the windows as the seasons pass by is not at all expected.'

To interact better with the surrounding city, the buildings are on stilts, leaving the ground floor free for gardens and communal activities, something rarely seen in the city. Laura is head of the Baboon communications agency, which includes design brands among its clients, while Francesco is a biologist and nature photographer. Laura was the most passionate about the house project because, as she explains, 'I come from a family that has been working with buildings and architecture for four generations.' To assist them in the renovation of the home, they turned to close friends at Eligo Studio. As Laura recounts, 'I've known Alberto Nespoli and Domenico Rocca, the two founders of the studio, for a long time, and I immediately thought that this project could suit them. I wanted to preserve the original features of the house, as, fortunately, it did not succumb to changing trends over the years. We sought a redevelopment of the existing project, updating the house according to our needs and tastes. Eligo has always maintained a very "cultural" approach to their projects: they never distort the spaces. On the contrary, they aim to recover and enhance what is beautiful, infusing it with contemporary solutions, sometimes even breaking with tradition, but always respecting the places.'

The result is a home that is eclectic and bright, contemporary yet timeless, and filled with art and plants. 'As for the jungle in the dining area?' asks Laura. 'The credit for this belongs to Francesco. We both love plants, but he is the one actually taking care of them. Having windows on all sides makes the space so sunny it could be a greenhouse, so it is perfect for growing tropical plants. We are particularly fond of our desert plants collection, various species of *Pachypodium* and *Adenium*. They remind us of our travels in Africa and the Middle East.'

'Having windows on all sides makes the space so sunny it could be a greenhouse, so it is perfect for growing tropical plants.'
– LAURA & FRANCESCO

Reinforcing the roots

HOMEOWNER
Alessandro Carrara

Florence is one of the cities that's on almost everyone's must-visit list. A hub of art and culture for centuries, the city still has narrow alleys that transport you to the Renaissance period. Besides the museums and architectural marvels, the city's historical wealth means that many grand palazzi still stand, offering the opportunity to create incredible contemporary homes.

For businessman Alessandro Carrara, his apartment is as much about the past as it is about his future. He explains, 'This is my place in the world, and my favourite part is the bedroom, with its jungle of plants drawn on the wall. It always keeps my feet on the ground and reminds me of what I do and where I come from. My family has been in the paper industry in Tuscany and Europe since 1873, and I find myself continuing what can be called a real passion and tradition for paper. The choice made by the architect, my friend Cosimo, to insert a natural element such as that of the forest is not accidental, because it recalls the raw material from which our entire production process starts and which we are committed to protecting. The furnishing accessories and the masonry elements recall this tradition that pays homage to my past and to my working and familial present.' While architect Cristina Romiti handled the structural renovation, Cosimo Bonciani took care of the interior design and furnishings as his first special project. 'I started working on this house when I had not yet graduated, while I was still studying. So Alessandro, a good friend of mine, was literally my first client.'

The apartment is in the heart of Florence's historic Sant'Ambrogio district in a three-storey villa known as Villino Pellizzari, designed by architect Giacomo Roster between 1869 and 1870. The home is around 100 square metres and would have been the sleeping quarters of the original owners; the building is now divided into two properties. A spacious living and dining area connects seamlessly to a well-appointed kitchen and a practical service bathroom. Adjacent to this communal space is a luxurious double bedroom with an en-suite bathroom. The house strikes a balance between past and present in its decor. Cosimo, the driving force behind the design, expresses the goal of maintaining a timeless atmosphere despite the recent renovations. 'Our desire was for the house to feel timeless. We aimed for each object to carry a story,' explains Cosimo. Alessandro and Cosimo share a passion for contemporary art, evident in the inclusion of works by emerging and non-Florentine artists within the space. However, there is one piece closer to Alessandro's heart than any other – the iconic 1970s wicker armchair by Emmanuelle Pavone for Kok Maison. He explains: 'The chair became the cornerstone of the project. It is a piece I am very fond of because it belonged to my maternal grandmother, and we have worked hard on making the space around it suitable for her presence.'

Homes Decorated by Nature 71

'The chair became the cornerstone of the project. It is a piece I am very fond of because it belonged to my maternal grandmother, and we have worked hard on making the space around it suitable for her presence.'

– ALESSANDRO

An architect's home

HOMEOWNER
Domenico Rocca

As co-founder of a creative agency focused on interior design, Domenico Rocco was in the perfect position to create the home of his dreams. He found it situated in a nondescript building from the 1960s in the Isola neighbourhood of Milan, once a mixed-use area with lots of small industrial and artisanal workshops cheek by jowl with working-class residences. The architecture was sleek and featureless, unlike the heavily decorated turn-of-the-century palazzi closer to the centre of town. By the time Domenico found his home, the Isola area had become gentrified; it is now one of the city's top spots for night owls. Being on the third floor mitigates the street noise, but upon entering the home, you understand that the owner is someone with great taste and elegance. While the structure of the building is unremarkable, the homes are spacious and architecturally well planned, as Domenico explains: 'As I renovated the brilliantly lit apartment on the third floor, its entire look and character underwent a transformation. It became eclectic yet understated, with a touch of Milanese and international influences.'

To achieve his desired look, Domenico relied heavily on the team of interior designers and decorators at his creative agency, Eligo Studio, who 'have the sensitivity to develop tailor-made projects that represent key concepts of Italian style'. The floors throughout the house were given particular attention, as he explains: 'The main rooms played a starring role in this transformation. Resin, in unconventional colours and complemented by oak strips, was applied to create a decorative effect, effectively turning them into unique "carpets".' This added a level of customised detail which Domenico was used to working with in commercial projects; therefore, he was not afraid to include numerous bespoke elements like the ceiling-height doors with antique brass handles or the kitchen. As Domenico says, 'The kitchen, entirely custom-made in iron and wood, is surrounded by simple moss-green tiles. Antique cabinets elegantly coexist with custom-designed furniture, and vintage pieces seamlessly blend with contemporary elements. In the bathrooms, I opted for reclaimed cement tiles to introduce a touch of the twentieth century. These tiles are artistically complemented by chromatic resin accents on the walls.' The constant interplay between the old and the new has resulted in what Domenico calls 'a timeless aesthetic, where tradition, contemporaneity and global influences gracefully come together in this unique dwelling'.

Homes Decorated by Nature 77

'A timeless aesthetic, where tradition, contemporaneity and global influences gracefully come together in this unique dwelling.'

– DOMENICO

Art and Decoration

CHAPTER TWO

'A room should feel collected, not decorated.'

– ALBERT HADLEY

The homes in this chapter all focus on using decoration to bring nature into indoor spaces. Some homeowners have chosen to express their connection to nature by using wallpaper, often featuring oversized leaves and flowers, while others use colour or organic shapes. Regardless of the chosen solution, these homes are always bright and airy, with considerable effort made to allow natural light in. There are numerous interpretations of decorating with nature, like artist Sofia Cacciapaglia, who has adorned her walls with a magical field of flowers, painted in her style on recycled cardboard boxes. Whatever your taste might be, nature is always welcome in the home.

Invasion of the flying lampshades

HOMEOWNER
Alvaro Catalán de Ocón

Alvaro Catalán de Ocón is a Spanish product designer and entrepreneur based in Madrid. After initially graduating from business administration, he continued his studies in product design at the Istituto Europeo di Design, Milan, eventually graduating with honours in product design from Central Saint Martins, London. Alvaro is the creator of the PET Lamp, a now ten-year-old project born out of the need to draw attention to the mountains of plastic waste in Bogotá, Colombia, which uses the traditional weaving techniques of local artisans. This hugely successful project confirmed to Alvaro his commitment to the betterment of the environment. Today, Alvaro lives in Madrid with his daughter Sofia and their two birds, who roam freely in the plant-filled corridor which divides his home from his studio.

Alvaro found the apartment two years ago while looking for a bigger studio space. It was in complete ruins, but Alvaro had a great feeling about it. 'I needed more studio space. The place was a complete ruin when I got it, but I felt it had something special. The heart of the house is the living room,' he explains, 'an area that is very malleable and flexible for any use. It's like a big playground where we project films onto the wall, read, sleep and stay up chatting. On one end, I have my bedroom, and on the other is Sofia's bedroom, which was conceived as a contained space inside another space. There is everything she needs: a bed, a basin, a cupboard, shelves, a play area, a drawing table. It even has a top floor, as if it were a magical house on a tree.'

Though the home is painted white and has a cement floor, it is warm and filled with natural light. The nature of Alvaro's work and the materials he chooses to work with – often natural or recycled materials – have a strong message of environmental consciousness. A mass of PET Lamps hangs from the ceiling to form a canopy that is reminiscent of laden seed pods hanging from a tree. He has designed office chairs with flower motifs and a collection of rugs, Plastic Rivers, woven from recycled plastic waste yarn that portrays a series of aerial images of some of the most polluted rivers on the planet. The home is scattered with potted plants of all shapes and sizes, which, combined with the natural light, gives the impression of being outside of the city as opposed to in the centre of it. From the way he chooses to live to the projects he creates, it is clear that Alvaro is a friend of the planet.

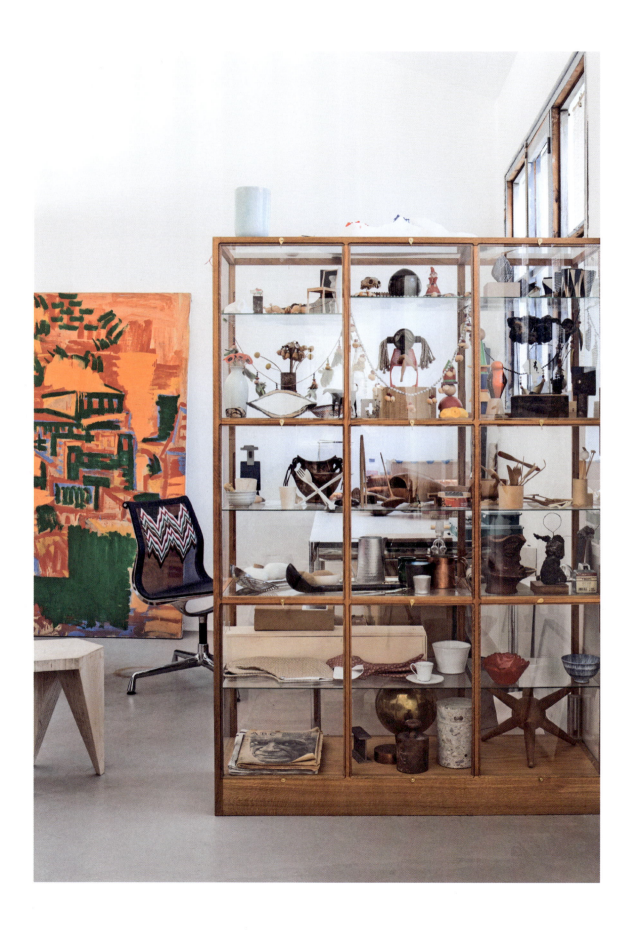

Art and Decoration

Homes Decorated by Nature

'The place was a complete ruin when I got it, but I felt it had something special.'

– ALVARO

Homes Decorated by Nature

Lucky number 40

HOMEOWNER
Frederik de Wachter

There is a joke that circulates within the city of Milan: if you threw a stone anywhere in the city, you would hit an architect. These days, you could also add a photographer and a designer to that joke. The city has long been a magnet for creative people, not just from within Italy, but from around the world. Walking into any architectural practice, you will see a diverse array of faces, just like in any major capital. Belgian architect Frederik de Wachter got his first taste of Milan at the age of 22 while studying interior design in Ghent, benefiting from the Erasmus exchange programme. He returned to the city again after spending three years in Barcelona to work for Migliore+Servetto before partnering with Alberto Artesani to found DWA Interior Architecture, a studio that today collaborates with numerous fashion brands. His transfer to Milan was nearly complete – Frederik needed a home.

After visiting close to 40 apartments, Frederik finally found what he was looking for on his birthday, the 11th of February, his lucky day. The size, position and style were all what he had been looking for. The home has all the details you would expect to find in a turn-of-the-century property: high ceilings, tall glass doors that allow in light and wind, plaster mouldings and ornate interior doors. The only thing not right was the herringbone parquet floor, which had been ruined, so Frederik opted for resin. As he explains, 'The floor was unsavable, and cement resin seemed like a choice that would open the space up in the right colour. I started off with grey, but I gradually felt the need for something lighter, and eventually it became white.'

While the home is restored with a high level of finish that elevates the original details, Frederik has made it his own by injecting the space with well-studied colours. Where the walls were white, he used fabric and pattern, while in the smaller, more intimate spaces, he used colours taken from nature – earth tones in the bedroom, dark salmon pink in the kitchen and dark blue reminiscent of a moody night sky. Despite Frederik's perception of his home decor as a spontaneous blend rather than a meticulously curated collection, it actually comprises a thoughtfully chosen array of distinctive pieces. From the iconic blue Rietveld armchair to the Albini table, the red Vico Magistretti chairs to the black Charlotte Perriand chair, each item has been meticulously selected. To bring life and nature into the space, almost every room has potted plants, lovingly taken care of by their owner. With his home, Frederik's transformation into a full Milanese is complete. Welcome, Frederik!

Art and Decoration

'The floor was unsavable, and cement resin seemed like a choice that would open the space up in the right colour.'

– FREDERIK

Homes Decorated by Nature 105

Escape to the country

HOMEOWNER
Delphine Bekaert

There is something romantic about the idea that you could someday radically change the direction of your life, breaking free from the path you've set for yourself and moving to a sunny climate with great food and rich culture, living life at a more human pace. For Delphine Bekaert, that meant leaving a successful career as an art gallerist in Ghent, Belgium, where she founded the Hoet-Bekaert Gallery with her former husband Jan Hoet in 2003. She moved with her daughter Lucy to a reconstructed farmhouse in Serranova, Apulia, on the Adriatic coast of Italy, a beautiful part of the world. 'The choice of living in Apulia was dictated by the desire to break away from the hectic working world in the art field and to embrace a new path that would allow me to have more time for what I love,' explains Delphine. 'It has been a very big change.'

When Delphine first saw the property, it required a lot of imagination to see the hidden gem below where the roof once was. 'We were looking for a place with a story. When I saw this land and this old building, I immediately fell in love with the facade and the old farmhouse, with its vaulted structure,' she explains. The restoration was going to be vast but would reflect the rural origins of the home, as well as the new occupants' love of design. 'Together with Jan, we decided to rebuild most of the house. The upper part was a roofless ruin. Everything else, from the interior to the roof, is new. Jan and I have combined our ideas. He is a genius – he manages to understand how to allow as much light in as possible and all the best ways to gain space,' says Delphine. 'Here we have a large kitchen, a living room, a bedroom, a room with a fireplace and a TV for our relaxation or for guests, a bathroom and, on the mezzanine, a terraced room for Lucy. Below, there are the caves.'

Part of the original stone construction, the caves add four more large rooms, which Delphine uses to create her D E L F I N ceramics range and where she can transform a love of collecting ceramics into designing and producing her own (www.delfinceramics.com). In contrast to the ancient caves, the bright white new addition to the home emphasises the constant dialogue with the outdoors. The black-framed windows are maximised, not just to allow in light and air, but also to invite you to enjoy the sight of the wild yet manicured garden, so lovingly designed by Delphine and Jan. Delphine adds, 'My house is always open, so my friends can enjoy the relaxed, informal atmosphere and nature on our doorstep.'

'We were looking for a place with a story. When I saw this land and this old building, I immediately fell in love with the facade and the old farmhouse.'

– DELPHINE

The secret garden

HOMEOWNERS
Cyrielle Rigot and Julien Tang

There are some places you visit that remain with you long after you've returned home, places that linger in your thoughts for months and beckon you back at every opportunity. For Parisian couple Cyrielle Rigot and Julien Tang, Marrakesh became that place after a holiday in 2010. 'Initially captivated by the light, which appealed to the photographer in Cyrielle, we spent the next four years visiting as often as possible. We travelled the entire country by car or motorcycle,' says Julien, an artistic director. 'We used to come regularly on holidays, and it became almost an obvious decision for us to settle here, despite not knowing another person living here!' Life in Paris had run its course, and the two creatives left the world of fashion behind to start a new life in the Red City.

After months of searching for their perfect home, navigating the maze that is the Marrakesh medina, they found a discreet passageway leading to what would become their refuge. 'We pushed open the two grand cedar doors that led us to the sumptuous and intimate palace we now call home. Here, organic elements and ornamentations come together in the most authentic expression of Moroccan architecture. Magic unravels. Time stops.'

The pair meticulously renovated the early twentieth-century Marrakesh residence, revitalising its vibrant mosaic tiles and stucco walls. Leveraging their background in fashion and design, they have infused the interiors with 1970s-inspired flair. Julien explains: 'Our decorating aesthetic is based on simplicity and sincerity. Fashion has taught us a sense of detail, the harmony of colours and how to mix fabrics – it helped us create a place that feels like our own little universe. We love to mix vintage elements with a touch of exoticism or with other forms and materials, for an eye-catching effect. Our goal was to achieve a timeless quality that we reinterpreted with elegant interiors and juxtaposed stylistic periods.' The couple utilised local artisans to create much of the furniture, while many items were found in flea markets around the city.

What makes this place truly special is the central courtyard, the epicentre of the riad. Here, a large fountain is surrounded by lush palms, even hosting some turtles. The contact with nature is constant and ever-present, whether it's finding shade from a tree or the smell of blossoms wafting into one of the six bedrooms. The couple has named the place Riad Jardin Secret, 'The Secret Garden', not only because it is an oasis hidden from the bustling city, but also because the home was reported to have belonged to a well-known Marrakeshi who kept it as a secret place to entertain his lovers.

'Our goal was to achieve a timeless quality that we reinterpreted with elegant interiors and juxtaposed stylistic periods.'

– CYRIELLE & JULIEN

Big, bold & beautiful

ARCHITECTS
Marcante-Testa

For Milan-based architecture and interior design studio Marcante-Testa, this apartment renovation posed several challenges. The 150-square-metre home was commissioned for a family, and structural changes to the layout were deemed unnecessary to save both time and money. With the building featuring an interior garden and windows on both sides, the studio aimed to bring nature into the project as much as possible: 'The visual relationship with nature was the guiding motivation behind the choice of this place on the part of the client, a place with which to identify and establish a personal rapport.' Despite Milan being a relatively green city, having the ability to see tree branches so close to every window is considered a real luxury.

The project, dubbed *Le Temps retrouvé*, or 'Time Regained', by the award-winning Marcante-Testa, resulted in a space that is contemporary yet old-fashioned. The studio states, 'The materials – like wicker, Vienna straw and linen that form seats, accessorised dividers, wardrobe doors, the fake-marble laminate of the kitchen table, the wicker headboards of the beds – join forces to evoke memories of spaces, perhaps experienced in a "grandmother's house", reinterpreted here and rendered functional for contemporary needs.' The use of natural materials, combined with nature-themed wallpaper and a delightful colour palette for the walls, brings joy into the space. When combined with abundant sunlight, it creates an atmosphere of a home to be enjoyed.

The numerous bespoke furniture pieces designed by Marcante-Testa – such as the kitchen and bathroom cabinets and the green divider cabinet with wicker back – update the space with a modern touch, and maintain a certain hardness and angularity. To complement these geometric pieces, the studio has incorporated mid-century vintage furniture, contributing to the narrative of a grandmother's house. One of the studio's strengths is its ability to create a continuous relationship with the outside world. A prime example is the dining room wall covered in Chiavi Segrete wallpaper from the Fornasetti II Collection by Cole & Son, hung on either side of the full-height glass doors. The interaction between the high swaying branches outside and the lush green wallpaper is striking and beautiful. The presence of the 1950s stone fawn and the mountain lion staring back at you adds a touch of pure irony.

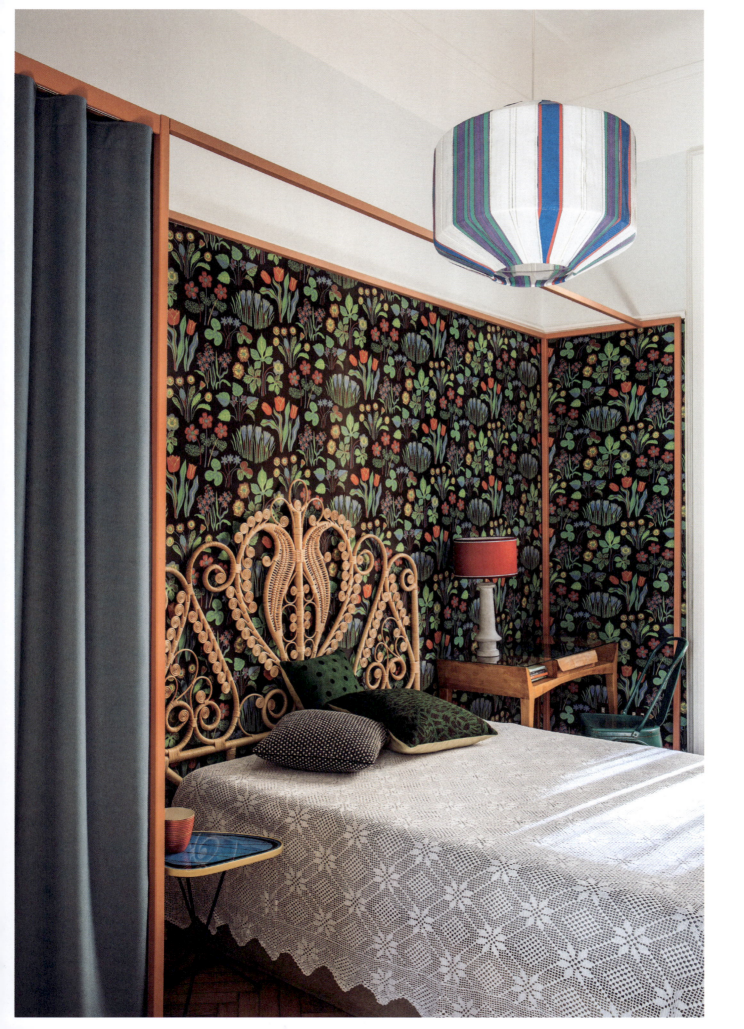

Homes Decorated by Nature 135

'The visual relationship with nature was the guiding motivation behind the choice of this place on the part of the client.'

– MARCANTE-TESTA

The return of the native

HOMEOWNER
Nicolas Lefebvre

'Not all those who wander are lost,' wrote J.R.R. Tolkien in *The Fellowship of the Ring*. While they may not be lost, the wanderer at a certain point returns home. For the unique French artist Nicolas Lefebvre, that home is in Paris and tells the story of Nicolas's many travels, both real and imagined.

His art is inspired by the Surrealist and Dadaist movements but is unique in its expression. As he moves through life, whether at home or abroad, he searches for objects – man-made artefacts, things from nature or pieces of scrap, possibly discarded, often precious – and then reconstructs these elements, crafting enigmatic and symbolic sculptures, into totemic figures that evoke the sacred. Like his work and his home, Nicolas has an air of having seen a lot. His shoulder-length hair and full beard frame an angular, sun-weathered face, and he dresses like a man who lives on a sailboat, the quiet, shabby elegance of those who know.

Situated among the rooftops of the 11th arrondissement, the building serves as both his home and his studio, as Nicolas explains: 'In my house, there are many elements that inspire my works, but the house is not intended as an extension of my studio, even if they are somehow connected.' The studio is made up of a series of small dormers, once the *chambres de bonne* of a Haussmannian building designed by one of Nicolas's ancestors. In contrast, the home is made up of a series of interconnected open spaces, with a sloped roof and lots of skylights and windows. The decoration is generally bohemian, with a mix of styles, periods and origins, telling the story of a man who is an adventurer, having lived in Peru, got lost in the Sahara Desert and roamed throughout India, like others before him. 'I studied art,' explains Nicolas, 'but I never thought of becoming an artist. Maybe a collector or a merchant. People led me in this direction, those who gave value to my works, a value that I could hardly recognise. Or, perhaps, I have fulfilled my dad's wish for himself: while aspiring to be an artist and despite having the talent, he has worked in another branch.' Nicolas likes to keep his art and his objects close to him, with seemingly every wall or space covered by some found or created piece. Some areas are naturally more crowded than others, but when he needs a break from it all, he has a space to get away. As he explains, 'There are plenty of relaxing and contemplative corners in the house, but the terrace is definitely my favourite place. I grew up in a very classic house, different from the one where I live now. But my sweet home reflects important moments of my life.'

Homes Decorated by Nature 143

'My sweet home reflects important moments of my life.'

– NICOLAS

Sofia's choice

HOMEOWNER
Sofia Cacciapaglia

Sofia Cacciapaglia is a painter and a native Milanese. After living in New York and London following her graduation from the renowned Brera Academy, she returned to her hometown and found a home that is absolutely *milanesissimo*. An internal courtyard with former laboratories can be found on the ground floor, while homes on the upper floors overlook the spacious cortile. Initially, in search of a workspace, she found a large studio with high ceilings and tons of space, a former laboratory housed in an eighteenth-century building, reached by traversing a large courtyard in the shadow of a huge palm tree. This is the beautiful side of Milan hidden behind the facades of a busy and lively street, where allure, bohemia and traditional crafts coexist. Once settled in, she knew she had to find a home in the same building. The available apartment was perfect for her and her husband Michael Eagleton, who works in finance. 'My first thought was: "Let's move in and enjoy this house exactly as it is with its 1960s atmosphere; we could easily be in Tuscany or Sicily." I love the worn terracotta floors, the central room without windows and the main staircase which is simply magical. I feel that it is an eloquent space, capable of expressing itself. I could have painted the walls, but then I would have conformed it to many other houses.'

The decision to leave the apartment in its 'run-down' state and to leave all the interior details untouched gives the home a sense of drama and romanticism, not unlike Sofia and her art. Her expansive canvases showcase otherworldly figures – women with unwavering gazes engaged in propitiatory rituals or adorned in ceremonial dresses and surrounded by fluttering flowers. Set against backdrops resembling idyllic gardens, these scenes transport viewers to an imaginary paradise. In 2019, the cavernous space of her studio inspired a seminal work of her career, *Locus Amoenus*, an immersive work that appears to grow from walls, around arches and through doorways; a wild, wind-blown, fantastical garden full of movement and colour; a collage meticulously painted on reclaimed cardboard that has hints of Klimt and the Orient. 'There is an environmental message in the use of this material, which, in my opinion, is very elegant, with a beautiful colour and a material that allows you to work quickly,' she explains.. 'I am a figurative artist, that's for sure. I feel very close to my works: they reflect my emotions, even if they are the result of a process of pure fantasy. All my subjects, whether they are women, flowers or figures, eventually become abstract.'

Homes Decorated by Nature 149

'Let's move in and enjoy this house exactly as it is with its 1960s atmosphere.'

– SOFIA

Homes Decorated by Nature 151

Conserving tradition

HOMEOWNER
Lúcio Rosato

Nestled within the enchanting historical quarters of Lanciano, a picturesque town in the province of Chieti, stands a residence that seamlessly weaves together the threads of tradition and modernity. The palazzetto, located on the busy Corso Roma, serves as the ancestral home of architect Lúcio Rosato. Born in this charming town, Lúcio has a connection to Lanciano that runs deep. As he recalls, 'It's my father's original village, where I was born, where we lived before we moved to Pescara.' Constructed in the early eighteenth century, this three-storey house spans approximately 350 square metres and boasts a classic square layout with an internal courtyard. What makes this dwelling particularly intriguing is its journey from abandonment to revival, with Lúcio overseeing the renovation project from the early 1990s. This project not only breathed new life into the structure, but also preserved its authentic character. 'When we entered in 1992, it had been uninhabited for decades, and despite various renovations, the precious original brick floors (completely darkened by time) had remained intact. I noticed them immediately – linseed oil and elbow grease brought them back to their ancient splendour,' says Lúcio.

As an architect deeply attuned to the marriage of form and function, Lúcio approached the restoration of the palace with a keen sense of purpose. The decorations on the ceilings, towering over 4 metres high, are not the only works of art. 'This palace is a kind of a gigantic storage space. My father – who, like my mother, was a writer and a poet – was also a collector. Paintings and sculptures by Abruzzo artists from the last century come from his gallery in Pescara.' From his great-grandparents, who were cabinetmakers, Lúcio inherited beautifully carved furniture. Having been mentored by artistic luminaries Ettore Spalletti and Franco Summa, his creative vision extends beyond mere aesthetics. The house, now a canvas for his artistic sensibilities, hosts 14 rooms that showcase not only his architectural prowess, but also a collection of his own artworks. Through thoughtful design and a meticulous restoration process, the palazzetto emerged as a harmonious blend of the old and the new, a testament to Lúcio's commitment to preserving Lanciano's historical charm while infusing it with contemporary vitality. As he explains: 'After all, change is intrinsic to my idea of the present. Who said that to preserve, we cannot modify? The concept of identity is also that of evolution.' He continues: 'My house is always different. It changes every day, influenced by light, moods and the desires of those who inhabit it. It accompanies and supports me; it transforms with me. In the end, that's what an architect must do: make people's lives more authentic.'

Homes Decorated by Nature 161

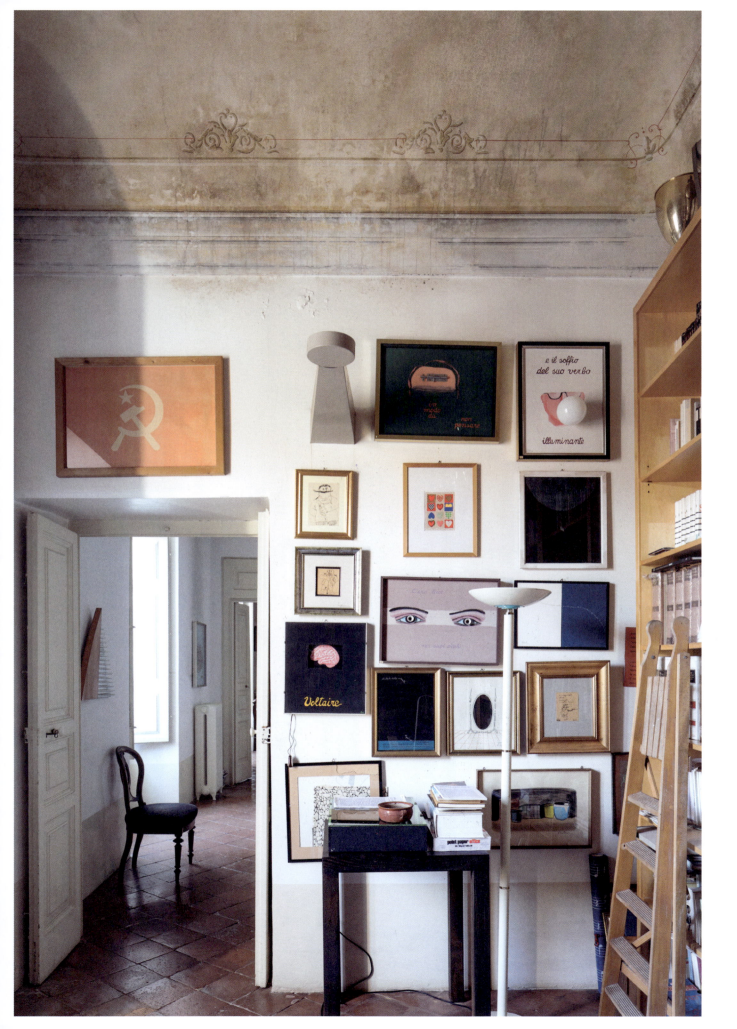

Homes Decorated by Nature 163

'Change is intrinsic to my idea of the present. Who said that to preserve, we cannot modify?'

– LÚCIO

Materials and Textures

CHAPTER THREE

'The Sun does not realize how wonderful it is until after a room is made.'

– LOUIS KAHN

The homes in this chapter are all about the natural materials and how to visually layer them to maximise their impact. Whether it is wood, stone or leather, our relationship with these materials dates back to our days of living in caves, whether in the form of stone-carved arrowheads or wooden clubs – strong and lightweight. Today, we value these materials differently, and often it's a case of 'the older, the better'. Who does not love a well-worn leather sofa from the 1970s or an old wooden farm bench, dry and gnarly, bleached by the sun? When working with natural materials, the biggest advantage lies in the tactile experience – the warmth of the surface, the unevenness of the cracks or veins. These are feelings that come from deep within, and as a rule of thumb, when something feels good, it will inevitably look good, too.

A surprising country home

HOMEOWNER
Samuele Failli

For talented footwear designer Samuele Failli, it was very important to have a home that would serve as a refuge from the rest of his life, which can be extremely hectic. Over the years, Samuele has collaborated with some of the biggest names in the luxury business, including Prada, Azzedine Alaïa and Yves Saint Laurent. So, when he arrives home to his two dogs, he needs to feel at peace. As Samuele says, 'I have found my perfect escape from the hectic routine. Every time I come home after my business trips, I feel like I am finally safe from stress.' This might seem a certainty given the 360-degree view of the Tuscan countryside, but it was not always like this. There was a huge amount of work that had to be put in to create this elegant and surprising country home. 'The first time I saw it, the building was in a state of total abandonment,' explains Samuele. 'So much so that some of the original decorative elements were hidden. The charm of an abandoned place, oozing with history, immediately persuaded me to choose this place as my home, although I was well aware of all the work that would be necessary to undertake to make my dream come true.'

It might be a house in the country, but once inside, it certainly is not your typical rustic farmhouse. Samuele enlisted the talents of Margherita Bacci and Cosimo Bonciani, two young architects who were just 25 years old at the start of this project. With the backing of Florence-based architectural firm Studio1 Architetti, they undertook a thoughtful and comprehensive renovation. The result was a significant transformation, breathing new life into the home environment while respectfully preserving its original structure. The interiors are fresh and contemporary, with bold choices of colour and pattern. The architects explain: 'We were committed to obtaining a very clean and linear scenography, from the choice of floors, with hand-nailed herringbone parquet or reclaimed floor tiles, to the walls and wooden beams, completely painted in white. In this way, the rich and colourful art and modern antiques in Samuele's collection stand out harmoniously, avoiding unwanted overlaps.' Constructed in 1721, the home is developed over three floors, where the ground floor has a dual use: on one hand, it is a welcoming space for guests; on the other, it is an intimate zone, with the study rooms and the kitchen, the latter with independent access. The first floor is Samuele's personal suite, a place dedicated to privacy where he can disconnect from the world. Here, too, the rooms are built as a succession; linked by the colour blue, they are tinged differently in the bathroom, the boudoir (with a precious wallpaper from the 1930s) and the sleeping area. Then there is the attic, dedicated to music and video, with a guest bedroom and a bathroom that hides a small bathtub under the roof. As Samuele explains, 'The final effect is outstanding, since each room has a mood of its own. Looking out the windows, I see only countryside and tiny villages in the distance. It all creates a unique contrast: a villa that looks like something out of Palm Springs which is instead immersed in the Tuscan landscape.'

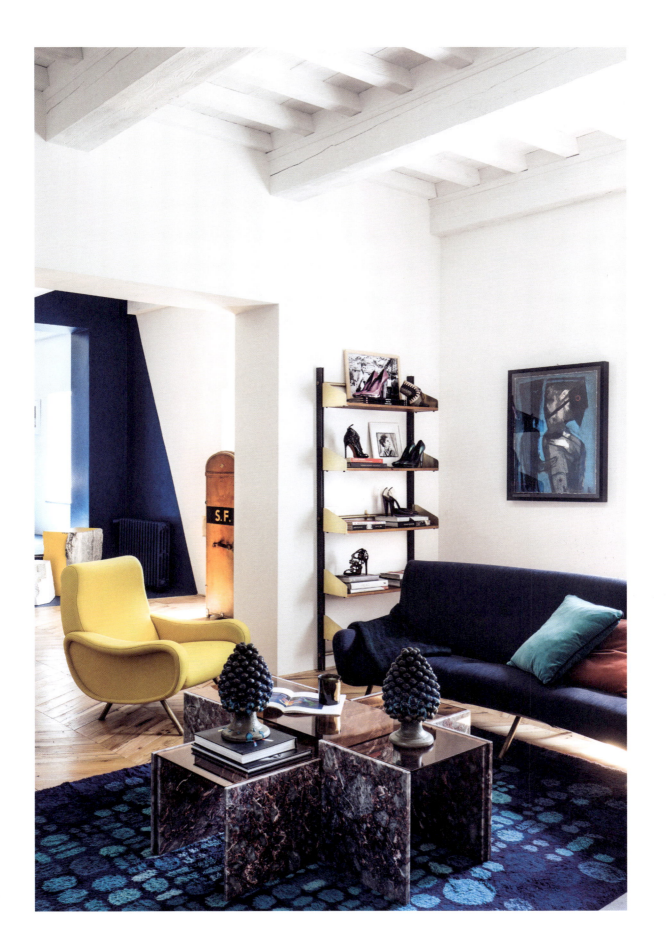

Homes Decorated by Nature

'The charm of an abandoned place, oozing with history, immediately persuaded me to choose this place as my home, although I was well aware of all the work that would be necessary to undertake to make my dream come true.'

– SAMUELE

Homes Decorated by Nature 177

Mid-century California style

HOMEOWNER
Davide Rizzo

Nestled in the hills of northern Abruzzo, surrounded by some of the most picture-perfect countryside, sits a home that appears to have been teleported from the Hollywood Hills. This is architect Davide Rizzo's Los Angeles–inspired 1950s bungalow, a little piece of paradise when he is not in Berlin, where he is based. 'I'm originally from the Como area in the north of Italy but spent a lot of time in the Abruzzo region when I was a child. My background is in architecture and interior design, with a particular love for the mid-century LA Hills style. I spend a couple of months in California every year and decided that I wanted to recreate something similar in Italy. In fact, the area where the villa is located has been nicknamed "Little California", so it was the perfect place to build a bungalow in the mid-century LA style,' explains Rizzo.

Set against a backdrop of olive groves, vineyards and the proximate allure of the Adriatic coast, the home becomes a sanctuary within an unspoiled natural expanse. After taking numerous trips to see the property, Davide finally took the steps to purchase the land and began planning his holiday home. Due to the fact that there were no restrictions placed on the style of the construction, Davide was free to design whatever he thought was best. 'I felt free to think differently from what I would normally do when designing houses and to build a mid-century-style home, reminiscent of Californian or Brazilian mansions with large windows framed in wood,' says Davide, who also designed the inner courtyard with palm trees and shrubs, creating a lush and almost exotic environment. The 180-metre-square building houses a large indoor and outdoor kitchen, a dining room and living room, two bedrooms with adjoining bathrooms, and a laundry and storage room. Below the pool area, there is an extra guest room with an en suite bathroom. The interior design of the space is characterised by an eclectic style, affording the flexibility to interchange individual pieces and seamlessly blend them with others whenever he wants, avoiding adherence to a singular aesthetic.

Throughout every room, the prevalence of contemporary artworks stands as a testament to Davide's deep-rooted passion for art. Annually, he extends invitations to artists, granting them a month to reside within the space; in return, they leave behind an artistic creation. Light is an important element in making art, and it was also a starting point for Rizzo. As he says, 'Light was very important to me when I did the design. Being oriented towards the mountains to the north, the property is what I call an "evening house" with an incredible sunset.' All the rooms have large sliding-glass doors that open onto a terrace with a pool and the incredible landscape in the background. 'I love taking in the lush views of the surrounding nature and stepping from the bed to the pool for a refreshing morning swim,' says Rizzo. 'Although it's also sensational to watch the sunset as you dive into the crystal-clear waters.'

Homes Decorated by Nature   189

'Light was very important to me when I did the design. Being oriented towards the mountains to the north, the property is what I call an 'evening house' with an incredible sunset.'

– DAVIDE

The perfect second home

ARCHITECTS
Bongiana Architetture

For many of us caught up in the daily rat race, fighting over every bit of cheese, a second home in the nearby countryside is a dream – who wouldn't love to be able to pack your car on Friday evening and be at your own dinner table for supper, then sleep over on Sunday and still make it in to work on time on Monday morning. For one Paduan family, the dream is a reality. Architects Pietro Bongiana and Silvia Codato from Bongiana Architetture had known the family for some time, and when taking them to view the property, expectations were not very high – the place was seriously run down and in need of a major renovation. But the viewing was a success, and soon the architects were planning the transformation of this derelict farmhouse into, as they explain it, a 'house not necessarily made to live in, but to be used for entertaining friends, sharing long days in the open air, and taking pleasure in being together'.

With the family living in nearby Padua, this would be their weekend getaway and summer refuge, close to home but far enough away in the countryside to forget where they were. For the architects, the first stage was having the building converted from agricultural to residential use. The second stage was the painstaking process of weaving together an incredible home for their clients.

'Our approach is grounded in the belief that listening to the client is the initial step in any project,' explain the architects. 'The house's transformation entailed a delicate blend of restoration and elimination. Attic areas were selectively removed to grant certain spaces a more expansive, double-height ceiling. The introduction of walkways facilitated access to the first-floor rooms, while the decision to preserve exposed brick walls harmonized with newly plastered surfaces. This form of architecture doesn't aim for indelible imprints but revels in playfulness, follows threads of irony and pursues a lightness that occasionally entices us, all while maintaining meticulous compliance with regulations. It embodies a playful ethos and a quest for freedom.'

While the original exposed red brick is the most ubiquitous material, it is the outdoors which most characterises the home. Right outside the door lies the heart of the countryside, with the Brenta river flowing nearby, flanked by fields of canola (rapeseed) that burst into vibrant yellow hues seasonally. The architects have installed as many windows throughout the home as possible, opening up the rustic yet elegant interior spaces to the vibrant outdoors. This truly is the second home of which dreams are made.

Homes Decorated by Nature 197

Homes Decorated by Nature   199

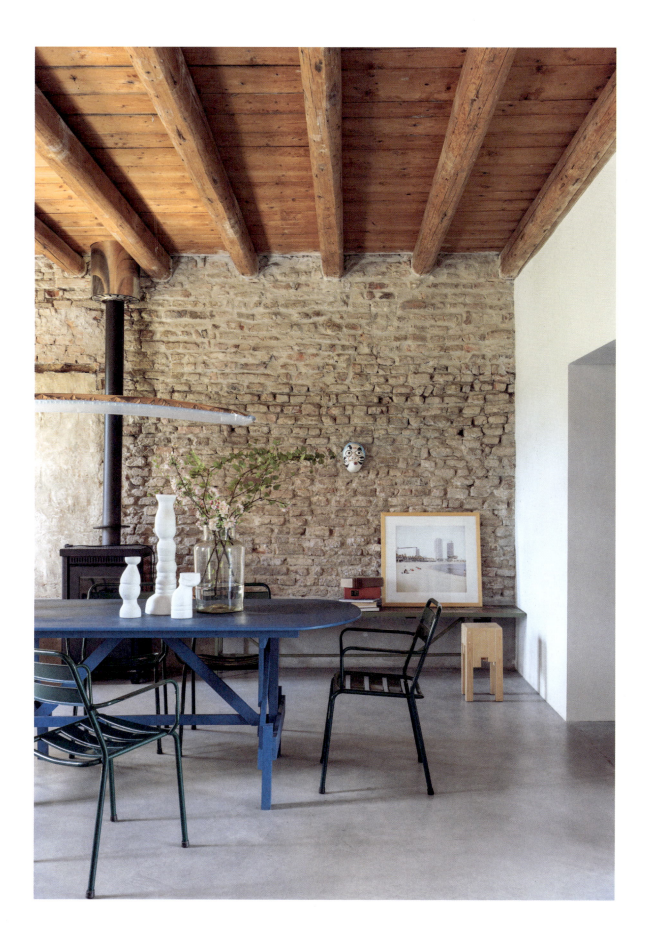

'This form of architecture doesn't aim for indelible imprints but revels in playfulness, follows threads of irony and pursues a lightness that occasionally entices us, all while maintaining meticulous compliance with regulations.'

– BONGIANA ARCHITETURRA

The stage is set

HOMEOWNERS
Pablo López Navarro
and Íñigo Aragón

Madrid residents Íñigo Aragón and Pablo López Navarro recently celebrated their twentieth anniversary as a couple. Since 2012, they have been partners in their design studio, Casa Josephine. After earning degrees in art history, fashion design and photography from their respective universities, they now operate as a cohesive team, seamlessly integrating design and cultural tradition into every project they undertake. Their portfolio spans diverse domains, encompassing both residential and commercial spaces. When they discovered this apartment in an old convent, the pair was delighted by the challenge to make it their own. Luckily, what they found was not in bad shape. As Pablo explains, 'You're probably expecting me to tell you how bad it looked. And how many tonnes of rubble we had to remove. Unfortunately, I can't help you with that. The flat was extremely well renovated. We took it straight away. It used to be a convent. Look at the passageway and see how thick the walls are. Íñigo and I have a vaulted ceiling in every room, which is really very special. We were able to focus entirely on the interior. That's our favourite thing to do anyway, so we're constantly changing everything [laughs]. In two months' time, it could look completely different here again.'

For the couple, it was the location as much as the property that attracted them, and they love the pace of life in the neighbourhood. 'La Latina is the oldest part of Madrid. The streets are narrow; they run crookedly up the hill, and there is a small square in front of our house. We have lots of bars and restaurants. And it's only a five-minute walk to the Palacio Real,' they say. With very little interior restoration to do, the couple really emphasised creating an atmosphere that reflected them as a couple. The walls are limewashed, which instantly gives the apartment an Ibizan or Greek feel, which is what they wanted – a space in the city that feels as though it could be a holiday home. What is very metropolitan is the artwork they have and the incredible two- and three-dimensional works they have in wood. As they explain, 'We art historians are terrible, I know [laughs]. We arranged the wooden figures in the library in the same way as the sculptures in the Parthenon pediments. But seriously, one of our favourite artists, the Italian Mario Ceroli, worked a lot with "manichini", or shadow figures; he is also a stage designer.' The theatrical theme recurs throughout, and a sense of drama permeates everything. 'We like that in the 70s, there were trends, particularly in Italian interior design, that emphasised the artificial arrangement, the staging. Or, you might say, the "stage-like". That was the high tide of postmodernism, where there were objects and furniture without any function. Like this wooden stele on which we placed an antique Roman portrait head. Or the library ladder in the corner that leads nowhere,' adds the couple.

'We were able to focus entirely on the interior. That's our favourite thing to do anyway, so we're constantly changing everything. In two months' time, it could look completely different here again.'

—PABLO & ÍÑIGO

Homes Decorated by Nature 211

Lord of the manor

HOMEOWNERS
Daniela Bennati
and Gianfranco Motter

Entrepreneurs Daniela Bennati and Gianfranco Motter embarked on a captivating journey in 2011 when they acquired a seventeenth-century manor house nestled in the serene village of Patú, Salento, on the south-eastern tip of Italy. The transformation of this historic dwelling into a tranquil haven unfolded with the creative guidance of architect Luca Zanaroli, culminating in a unique holiday retreat for the couple and their 11-year-old son Zoltan the following year. Having initially discovered Salento in 2008, Daniela and Gianfranco were captivated by the region's rich history, its idyllic location at the confluence of the Adriatic and Ionian Seas, and the picturesque olive trees that adorn a landscape in which Daniela fondly says, 'Each village is like a rare jewel.'

The village of Patú, with its agricultural heritage evident in subterranean silos once used for wheat storage, served as the ideal canvas for the couple's venture, with the manor itself standing in the grounds of an ancient underground olive mill. The couple's vision for the manor materialised through a meticulous refurbishment process, preserving and celebrating its architectural legacy. The stables, now transformed into a living area adjacent to an open-plan kitchen and dining space, hold a special place in Daniela's heart. 'It's our favourite room,' she shares. The ground floor further unfolds with a second kitchen, a dining room for entertaining guests, a reading room, a cloakroom and the main bedroom. Upstairs, Zoltan's bed, specially crafted by Zanaroli, fits snugly in a corner beneath the arching ceiling. The house exudes character, a testament to Daniela and Gianfranco's commitment to maintaining its architectural richness. Fireplaces dating back to the 1600s grace the kitchen, while intricately patterned flooring in the main bedroom and reading room infuses vibrant hues of green, yellow and ochre. Original windows, strategically placed high on the walls, bathe the interiors in natural light, creating a bright and airy ambiance.

Daniela and Gianfranco have added a curated collection of antiques and modern design pieces, which seamlessly integrate with the house's ambiance. Metal lights by Artemide cast a warm glow on an array of accessories sourced from local second-hand shops, including antique mirrors, ceramics and a repurposed stone drinking trough now serving as a bathroom washbasin. Beyond the walls, the couple has fashioned an inviting al fresco space for entertaining in the courtyard, complete with white concrete kitchen units and a generously sized built-in barbecue. This modern addition harmoniously complements the whitewashed exterior, creating an enchanting backdrop. For Daniela and Gianfranco, their Salento home signifies more than a residence: it is an escape, a haven where history and contemporary design seamlessly coexist, inviting both relaxation and celebration.

Homes Decorated by Nature

218　Materials and Textures

'Each village is like a rare jewel.'

– DANIELA

Homes Decorated by Nature

Urban oasis

HOMEOWNER
Andrea Mingotti

Milan is not known for its beauty; that superlative is generally reserved for Rome or Venice. In Milan, people come to work. This is mainly the result of post-war renewal and the Lombardy region being the industrial heart of the entire country. For years, there were light to medium industries producing goods within the city, and this home was built in a renovated shoe factory. When local architectural firm Mingotti e Giordano Architetti was appointed to oversee the conversion of the old factory into three commercial units, Andrea Mingotti saw an opportunity and purchased one of the units for himself. A resident of Venice, Andrea was in search of a pied-à-terre in Milan, and this loft made perfect sense. The space spans a generous 200 square metres with a square floor plan and two magnificent private courtyards. The first is at the entrance, guarded by a stylish 3-metre-high steel-and-glass gate, while the second is a sun-soaked paradise on the southern side that opens up to an inviting outdoor living space and a real luxury in the city – a pool.

Stepping into the main open space, you are met with 6.5-metre-high ceilings and a classic industrial shed roof with massive skylights that flood the interior with natural light. The flooring, a masterpiece in itself, boasts a handmade concrete surface meticulously restored to echo its original splendour, creating a seamless blend of heritage and contemporary design. As Andrea explains, 'The goal of the project was to preserve the industrial footprint. The load-bearing structures were left with layers of the original exposed paintings, treated with resin to preserve them.' However, the comparisons with an industrial style stop there. Andrea and his studio have created a slick contemporary home with a high level of finish and immaculate taste. Nestled in one corner is a walnut wood block measuring 5 metres square and standing 3 metres tall – an ingenious way of housing all the home's equipment and freeing up the external walls. The block also serves as a home to the wardrobe and master bathroom. As Andrea says, 'The "cube" was meticulously crafted and assembled at the workshop of the carpenter affiliated with our studio. It underwent rigorous testing and was then expertly dismantled and reassembled on site.' Concealed behind walnut panels outside are an array of storage compartments and kitchen essentials. An authentic 1940s bar counter adds a touch of elegance and vintage charm. Positioned above the 'cube', the primary bedroom boasts a serene ambience in light-grey hues, accentuated by a generously sized glass window on the roof, spanning 6 metres in length and 2 metres in height. When Andrea is in the city, he can return to this oasis in the city after a long day's work. As he recounts, 'My favourite place in this house is in summer when I'm in the garden – a real oasis of silent relaxation surrounded by green, but in the very centre of Milan.'

'My favourite place in this house is in summer when I'm in the garden – a real oasis of silent relaxation surrounded by green, but in the very centre of Milan.'

– ANDREA

Homes Decorated by Nature

Renovated farmhouse

HOMEOWNERS
Eva Noemi Marchetti
and Francesca Guarnone

For best friends and designers Eva Noemi Marchetti and Francesca Guarnone, living as close to nature as possible is fundamental to their creative process. Having met in high school, the two attended design university together in Milan, graduating with degrees in fashion and set design, which led to gaining experience with top set designers and luxury brands. As the world came to a grinding halt due to the pandemic, the friends decided they wanted a change in scenery and life in general. Originally hailing from Casteggio, a quaint village in Oltrepò Pavese, they opted for Trivolzio, situated near Bereguardo, a small locale close by. As the designers explain, 'We founded Studio Terre in 2020, in June. In the midst of the pandemic, we became aware of the direction we were going in and that we wanted something more real, something that would give us feelings of positivity. We were looking for a lifestyle and satisfaction that were closer to our ideals. Moving away from the chaos of the city to Trivolzio in the province of Pavia, close to nature and with a slower pace, we decided to set up our experimental art studio.' The two friends also have a third partner, Riccardo Brunetti.

A renovated group of farm buildings surrounded by working farms and ploughed fields would become their new home and studio, where they could fully express their creative philosophies and produce their one-off pieces in materials inspired by their environment. Each piece has a unique essence and narrative, crafted from sustainable materials such as clay and glass, connecting them to the history of the region while maintaining a seamless harmony with nature. As they say, 'We are guided by a deliberate, hands-on method, influenced by sunlight and the ebb and flow of seasons. Immersing ourselves in the tactile process and sculpting novel shapes is an integral aspect of the creative journey.' In the fields of Pavia, the studio subscribes to the philosophy of slow living. As they explain, 'Embracing slow living within our studio extends seamlessly to what we term as "slow design". Our focus revolves around crafting objects and environments that exude intimacy and personality, each narrating its own story through the investment of time and meticulous care. This approach is deeply rooted in the essence of Mediterranean living, drawing connections to our origins. From our perspective, there's a pronounced emphasis on the home and tradition. We believe there is significance in propagating the principles of "slow design" and cultivating awareness about the critical use of sustainable raw materials. The emphasis lies in acknowledging the time required to study and craft objects that align with the principles of sustainability and circularity – values more imperative in today's context than ever before.'

Homes Decorated by Nature

'Embracing slow living within our studio extends seamlessly to what we term as "slow design".'

– EVA & FRANCESCA

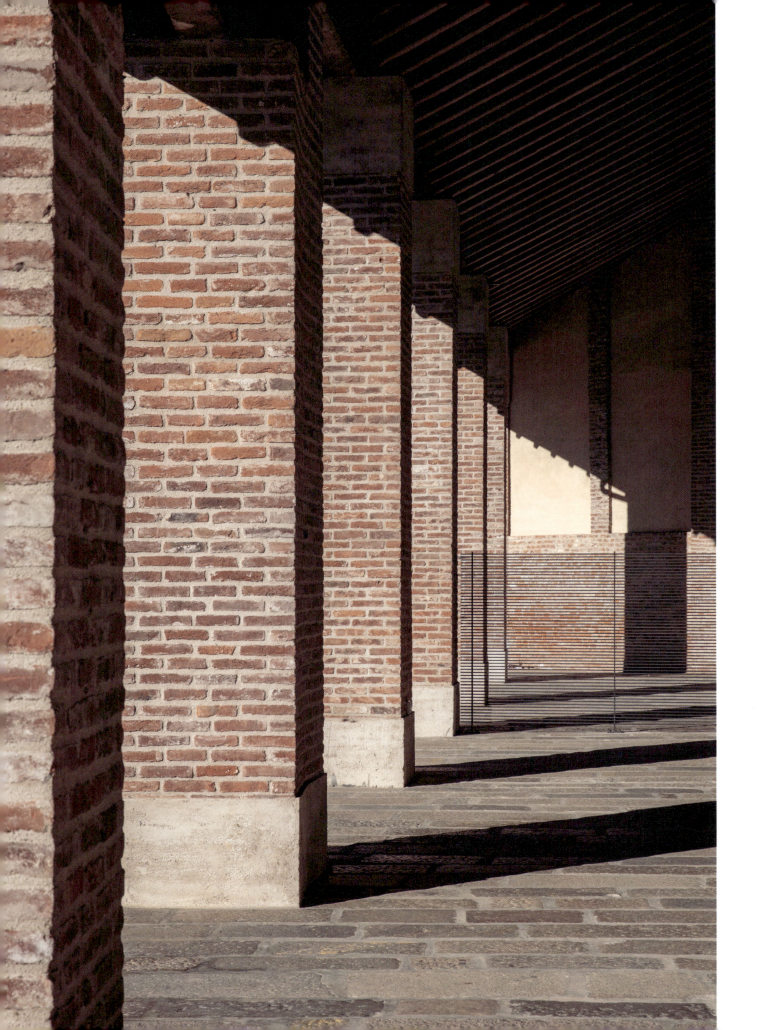

Homes Decorated by Nature 239

Bohemian atmosphere

HOMEOWNERS
David and Melina,
with Pedales the dog

A young woman in need of repairs to her bicycle goes in search of a repair shop. She is greeted by the handsome owner of the business, and once the bike is fixed, the two begin spending time together. Today, they are still together and have added a new member to their family, a terrier named Pedales. Melina was born in Mexico and was already an accomplished architect when she met David, a former lawyer who hung up his tie to open the bicycle workshop. The couple soon found that they had much in common: a passion for art, travel and design. However, their deepest connection is reserved for leather. Together, they founded leather workshop Oficio Studio, where they design and craft a wide array of leather products. Their production process is distinguished by a deliberate pace, resulting in impeccable details. 'We love doing things well; we love slow and traditional manual skills. We need to have so much patience to come up with unique high-quality pieces,' explains Melina. Making a bag is comparable to designing a house: you have to create a three-dimensional object where proportions, structure and material will hold only if they are in perfect balance.

To have enough space to produce their leather goods and save costs, they searched for a solution with a living space and working space in one. The couple found a mid-nineteenth-century building in the lively Barrio de las Letras neighbourhood of Madrid. As Melina explains, 'The apartment, on a third floor with a sunny terrace, was not at all in good condition. Yet we were fascinated by some details, like the large industrial glass windows and the decadent, bohemian atmosphere that one could breathe here. We were won over.' With much work to be done, the couple created a home that makes the most of the original structure – lots of windows, high ceilings and an original parquet floor that just needed to be brought back to life. The result is an eclectic open space with tons of natural light and the feeling of indoor forests created by a large number of potted plants. 'I love to take care of the plants; they remind me of the nature in Mexico, bringing a breath of life into the city,' she says. 'Even little Pedales (the couple's Parson's terrier) seems to appreciate the presence of plants; he sometimes smells them, hiding himself among the climbers in the living room.' The couple has constructed a perfect environment for themselves, with their workplace next to their home, and filled it with life-giving plants. But one cannot stay indoors all day, especially with Pedales. As Melina says, 'We like to break the day off with a visit to a café and a walk in the city centre with Pedales; it's an excuse to walk and live the neighbourhood life, which is extremely lively and creative. But the best thing here are the sunsets – from our windows, the views of Madrid are special. I can stop for hours to watch flocks of herons and storks flying to Africa in search of warmer weather.'

'We were fascinated by some details, like the large industrial glass windows and the decadent, bohemian atmosphere that one could breathe here.'

— MELINA

Homes Decorated by Nature

Homes Decorated by Nature 247

Brought back to life

HOMEOWNER
Enrico Serventi

Gentrification is a term frequently bandied about in today's major cities – out with the old and in with the new. It has happened in Tribeca in New York City and in Shoreditch in London; in Milan it's seen in Nolo, an area just north of the city centre boasting some of the city's finest historic buildings. For architect Enrico Serventi, a man of great taste, his residence in a 1905 palazzo presented an opportunity to revitalise a family home. As Enrico recounts, 'The spaces were in an advanced state of decay due to a poor 1950s renovation that had not been updated since. There was no heating system, except for a hazardous gas stove. The wooden floors were rotten, and the fixtures were poorly placed. What captivated me about the apartment, however, was the wonderful view of Trotter Park. I have three small balconies overlooking this green area, creating the sensation of being outside of Milan.'

The apartment underwent a complete restoration, with the internal layout revamped to suit a more contemporary lifestyle. The former main bedroom is now the kitchen and dining area, featuring an exposed beam ceiling typical of the period, but updated in a modern soft powder-white hue. The first of the three French doors perfectly frames the nature outside, while the marble slab on the wall is from a family property in the countryside. The space is immaculate in its colour palette, materials and finishing.

Moving from room to room, one follows a chromatic theme that is both refreshing and simultaneously dramatic. The lowered central corridor is a cool blue with a cement floor adorned with brass inlay, leading to the remaining three rooms of the house. The master bedroom is characterised by a dramatic Bordeaux entrance with heavy velvet curtains, impeccable furniture and a terrazzo floor. The remaining doors off the corridor lead to the study and the living room, with the lounge unquestionably being the most beautiful room in the home. Exposed blue ceiling beams and herringbone parquet distinguish the lounge from the other spaces; the furnishings are a mix of mid-century and classic design pieces blended with family heirlooms. As Enrico explains, 'The atmosphere of the house is typical Milanese from the early 1900s. Through the furniture and the use of colour, the space evokes eclectic influences of multiple styles and pigments, coexisting in balance. I wanted to restore dignity and identity to a house that over time had been distorted and deprived of its character. For example, the doors, the fireplace and the radiators are decorated in cast iron, and many of the marble surfaces come from family properties located in the Brescia countryside. If I had to choose my favourite room, it would be the living room, particularly the soft natural light which comes in from the outside and illuminates the fireplace, enhancing its shapes and geometries. I love the painting hanging over the fireplace: it is an artwork owned by my family, handed down for generations.'

'I wanted to restore dignity and identity to a house that over time had been distorted and deprived of its character.'

- ENRICO

Homes Decorated by Nature

Credits

IMAGES Helenio Barbetta
TEXT Kurt Stapelfeldt
BOOK DESIGN Elise Castrodale
EDITING Amy Haagsma

PP. 18-27, 44-55, 56-65, 74-83, 98-105, 138-145, 146-155, 194-203, 232-239 **STYLING** Chiara Dal Canto

Sign up for our newsletter with news about new and forthcoming publications on art, interior design, food & travel, photography and fashion as well as exclusive offers and events. If you have any questions or comments about the material in this book, please do not hesitate to contact our editorial team: art@lannoo.com

© Lannoo Publishers, Belgium, 2024
D/2024/45/330 - NUR 454/450
ISBN: 978-94-014-9554-7
www.lannoo.com

All rights reserved. No part of this publication may be reproduced or transmitted in any form or by any means, electronic or mechanical, including photography, recording or any other information storage and retrieval system, without prior permission in writing from the publisher.

Every effort has been made to trace copyright holders. If, however, you feel that you have inadvertently been overlooked, please contact the publishers.